DESTRUCTION OF THE LOVER

Poems by Luis Panini

Translated by Lawrence Schimel

DESTRUCTION OF THE LOVER

Poems by Luis Panini

Translated by Lawrence Schimel

PLEIADES
P R E S S

Pleiades Press Translation Series

Warrensburg, Missouri

Library of Congress Control Number:
ISBN 978-0-9970994-3-0

Published by Pleiades Press

Department of English
University of Central Missouri
Warrensburg, Missouri 64093

Distributed by Small Press Distribution

Cover Image:
Book design by Sarah Nguyen

First Pleiades Printing, 2019

Financial support for this project has been provided by the University of
Central Missouri and the Missouri Arts Council, a state agency.

Contents

Tu me tues.
Tu me fais du bien.
–Marguerite Duras, *Hiroshima mon amour*

DESTRUCTION OF THE LOVER

INTRODUCTION

A young man engages in a clandestine love affair with another man. It must remain a secret because the social or political climate is hostile to such a passion and will not grant it permission to unfold or be expressed in the open. Or maybe it's that other man who hasn't quite negotiated the pull of his desire—a pleasure he can indulge by ensconcing with his starry-eyed lover inside a cheap out-of-the-way hotel room, the noise of the television muffling the moans of ecstasy. Afterward, when they step out into the public light, they slip back into pretense, perhaps even erasure. That's where the story ends for the man who's comfortable with the closet: what is not seen or suspected did not happen. It cannot be named and therefore it will not be judged or criticized. Or remembered. No harm done.

But what of the young man who has been deeply affected by this experience, he for whom the carnal pleasure is not only physical gratification, but emotional need as well? For him, the story doesn't conclude as easily with the simple return of the hotel keys, not when he names this rendezvous a "romance." For him, the consummation of the sexual attraction is simply another paragraph in a narrative that some might call a relationship. What heartbreak for the young man to come to realize that his lover doesn't share such an amorous view of what has transpired. When the dust settles, a harsh clarity reveals itself: this was a short-term thing, a fantasy so shoddy it collapsed as soon as the sex was over. Now, "only the ruins remain." Evidence of damage, indeed.

Luis Panini pays homage to the loss of innocence that is akin to a rite of passage for the gay young man who confuses attention for affection, lust for love. We are told he's an adolescent. We know that he's a dreamer. And at various points in the narrative he comes across as intelligent, naïve, imaginative, gullible, vulnerable, careless, and eventually empowered by his journey through this emotional range. He comes to recognize the valuable take-away of the tryst: "You neither create nor destroy me, you only transform me." You, the lover. You, the circumstance. You, the avenue to queer life. As a declaration of growth and maturity, it is a hard-won statement, one that's accompanied by dejection and disappointment. But so too comes enlightenment.

The beauty of *Destruction of the Lover* is its daring homo-eroticism ("Like an arm entering the sleeve of a shirt, that's how my pinky disappears into your foreskin's many folds.") and its amplification of an experience that is usually relegated to silence or contained within the intimate circles of a queer communi-ty. Mostly these stories vanish because many do not have access to such friendships that can bear witness to the testimonies of same-sex love. I am reading this book, of course, through its Mexican cultural context, where religious and societal mores push homosexuality into the shadows. Hence, why some men choose to remain secretive and on the down low, feeding their personal hungers at the expense of those who yearn for sustenance and substance.

Thankfully, Panini doesn't present this story as a trag-edy. The comic moments don't allow it to become submerged into despair. The young man, savvy and even sassy, continual-ly makes clever, slightly campy pronouncements like this one describing anal sex: "The cross section that usually represents the reproductive system is the most inaccurate anatomical drawing because it never reveals the way in which the sphincter becomes an engagement ring." Though it's evident the young man uses humor to fortify his courage, what remains unspoken, at least for the moment, is the difficult truth of this arrangement: that he's deceiving himself into believing there's potential for more than a mere sexual encounter.

The reader will want to champion this young man's wish-ful thinking. We have all stood at that precipice at one time or another. We were young once and eager to enter the adventurous threshold of adulthood, uninhibited yet unfamiliar with the ways of the broken world. We were idealistic and unsullied, relatively unscarred. The sky, the ocean, and the landscape before us so vast that only opportunity could fill it. The young man takes this same anticipative lens to consider the body of his lover: "Your chest is a pair of mountains divided by an abysmal canyon and the abdomen a desert formed of identical dunes. A tundra extends across your face, like eternal winter, so white and ice-like. Your armpits guard the wetness of a tropical forest and your sex is a jungle of exotic animals and juicy roots, where it rains all year round."

And when the young man pleads with his lover, "Don't depart in such a hurry into the dark night. Stay here with me inside this cocoon. Because on the other side of that door one needs wings, stingers, and calloused extremities to defend oneself. Exoskeletons. On this side, we can just remain as larvae," we want to hug our younger, frightened selves. When the lover does leave, it is abandonment, a break-up, a wounding of the fragile heart.

But youth also has a saving grace—resilience. Though it comes with a cost. In this case, an eventual tearing away of the feelings from the soul, its unstitching painful but necessary. It manifests itself as grief ("I loaned you a white-and-blue checkered shirt. You gave it back to me impregnated with your sweat…I used to sniff it to calm myself down, until one day my mother stuck it in the washing machine."), as vindictiveness ("Dante forgot to chart in his Inferno the circle where metrosexuals will be punished."), as cynicism ("Honey, No one handed me a map to follow you into the forest where you roam unfettered. I'm losing your scent."), and finally, as spiritual cleansing ("I shall burn our bed tonight. Let no trace of us remain."), which will usher in the healing, or at the very least, the moving on. It's important to note, however, that with his final words the young man makes clear that he has transcended the turmoil and found solace in accepting the unfair but unequivocal position of the lover. For the young man, the episode is now history, but one that's preserved in a personal archive distant from the glare of shame and regret: "You and I will always retain an alphabet tattooed in scarlet ink beneath our clothes."

As a bittersweet story about love, the prose poems of *Destruction of the Lover* shatter the myth that such narratives are a thing of the past—not for the many who live outside of the privileged spaces where same-sex desire does not have to imagine or devise a language in order to exist. Panini's speaker becomes resourceful in order to breathe through the suffocating censure and invisibility imposed upon his truths. Testimony triumphs over angst. He comes away not unhurt, but not completely undone. Phoenix-like, he will rise from ashes, his heart recharged.

Panini's language sparkles with ingenuity, casting a dazzling new light over a relatable journey, and Lawrence Schimel's pitch-perfect translation captures the nuance of a speaker who's book-smart but still discovering the shape of his queerness.

—Rigoberto González

I.

Construction of the Lover

There are many names in history
but none of them are ours.
                    –Richard Siken, *Crush*

1.

Una estampa anatómica también es un mapa. La imagen de tu cuerpo impresa sobre la superficie blanca de un folio en el que estén debidamente ilustrados todos tus órganos, huesos y músculos, para comprender su milagroso ensamblaje.

1.

An anatomical diagram is also a map. The image of your body printed on the white surface of a page on which all of your organs, bones, and muscles are carefully illustrated, in order to understand their miraculous assembly.

2.

Estableciste el romance mediante un golpe que cimbró la vulnerabilidad de mi abdomen. Transmitir aquella desmedida violencia en ese cuarto de hotel fue la excusa perfecta para acercarte a mi cuerpo doblado, en busca de oxígeno, al nivel de la alfombra. Cuando aquel beso arrítmico tranquilizó al pánico pulmonar, entonces mis labios buscaron la ruta más rápida. En la garganta escurrió el sabor al que tarde o temprano se acostumbran los turistas fáciles cuando los sorprende el diámetro de la boca.

2.

You triggered our romance through a blow that shook the vulnerability of my abdomen. Imposing such excessive violence in that hotel room was the perfect excuse for you to approach my body, doubled over on the floor, striving for oxygen. When that arrhythmic kiss calmed the pulmonary distress, my lips then sought the fastest route. Down my throat dripped that taste which sleazy tourists get used to sooner or later when surprised by the diameter of the mouth.

3.

No necesitas tatuajes o lunares, perforaciones o cicatrices. Ninguna seña particular te hace falta porque me resulta muy fácil distinguir tu piel entre los animales desnudos.

3.

You don't need tattoos or moles, perforations or scars. Not a single distinguishing mark is required because it is quite simple for me to single out your skin from that of other naked animals.

4.

Un cuerpo encima de otro cuerpo. Así comenzó nuestra historia, ese *accidente*. No hizo falta verbalizar el deseo. Nos tomó un instante comprender que el lenguaje era una enfermedad de la garganta. Sin la necesidad de pronunciar un solo vocablo, la cama fue espejo, y la siguiente mañana nos devolvió una imagen que tuvo mucho de fósil: los dos calcados en alto relieve, las sábanas repujadas.

4.

One body atop another body. That's how our story began, *that accident.*
There was no need to pronounce our desire. It took us a moment to
understand that language was a sickness of the throat. Not needing to
speak a single word, the bed became a mirror, and offered us the next
morning an image that had much of a fossil to it: there, on the sheets,
were the two of us embossed in high relief.

5.

No queda espacio alguno en donde tu silueta musculosa no se pronuncie. No existe terreno en la faz del planeta cuyas variaciones topográficas no me recuerden las formaciones rocosas de tus gestos distintos. Según desde donde me observas, así reconozco tu rostro, todas sus fallas geológicas. Al arrugar el entrecejo cuando tratas de adivinarme en la distancia. Al desplomarte después de eyacular. Sismo de huesos, de carne, de barba que raspa.

5.

There is no place left where your muscular silhouette is not present. There is no land on the surface of the planet where topographical variations don't remind me of the rocky formations of your different gestures. Depending on where you observe me from, that's how I recognize your face, all of its geological faults. When you frown, when you try to distinguish me from the distance. When you collapse after ejaculating. Quake of bones, of flesh, of stubble that scrapes.

6.

Inventamos un sistema de códigos clandestinos capaz de aliviar el distanciamiento de nuestras lenguas. Por ejemplo, aquel guiño efímero y habitual se convirtió en un gesto bendito que justificó la eternidad de las horas. Algunos lo interpretaron como un rechazo al polvo del aire. Otros lo confundieron con la necesidad mecánica de humectar al globo.

6.

We invented a system of secret codes capable of alleviating the distance between our tongues. For example, that habitual and ephemeral wink became a blessed signal that justified the eternity of the hours. Some interpreted it as a rejection of dust in the air. Others took it as the mechanical need to keep the eye moist.

7.

Si somos discretos, si aparentamos casuales, podríamos desprendernos del gentío y acariciarnos detrás de un muro ciego. Aunque también un montículo de arena, o el tronco grueso de un árbol, podría ampararnos lejos de la luz mercurial. Nadie se va a dar cuenta. El eco de tus palabras deviene ciclos. Ora se escucha como las pisadas en vaivén de una fiera en cautiverio. Ora suena a canicas que rebotan dentro del cráneo.

7.

If we are discrete, if we act casual, we can distance ourselves from the crowd and caress one another behind some blind wall. Although a mound of sand, or the thick trunk of a tree, might also shelter us far from the mercurial light. Nobody will know. The echo of your words becomes cycles. Now I can hear it as the pacing to and fro of a beast in captivity. Now it sounds like marbles that bounce inside the skull.

8.

Al aire que inhalo lo filtra una almohada cuando la anticipación de tu lengua con su saliva dibuja una línea, la que forman mis vértebras. Un pincel deslizándose desde el altísimo occipucio hasta la Patagonia del cóccix.

8.

The air I inhale is filtered by a pillow when the anticipation of your tongue draws a straight line with saliva down my vertebrae, like a brush descending from the high occiput to the Patagonia of the coccyx.

9.

La nuestra también es la historia de un crimen. Enlistemos aquello que pueda comprometernos: mis huellas digitales tatuadas en la película de bronceador que te adereza la piel, los vellos púbicos enredados entre las muelas, restos de semen endurecido en el cabello, rasguños que la deshidratación de la piel hizo visibles, impresiones dentales en ambas clavículas, ADN a manos llenas. Ante la mirada de un experto forense, ¿cómo disimular la evidencia en esta habitación doble de hotel? Supongo que debe ser más sencillo engañar a este experto (el parentesco sanguíneo le venda los ojos). Ayúdame, vamos a deshacer la otra cama, a revolverle las sábanas. Simulemos que sobre esas almohadas también descansó el peso de una cabeza.

9.

Ours is also the story of a crime. Let's catalog what might compromise us: my fingerprints tattooed on the film of sun tan lotion that sheltered your skin, those pubic hairs tangled between molars, hardened remains of semen in the hair, scratches made visible by our dehydrated skin, my bite marks on both your clavicles, DNA just about everywhere. How can we hide the evidence in this double bed hotel room from the scrutiny of a forensic professional? I suppose it should be easier to fool this expert (family ties act as a blindfold). Help me, let's unmake the other bed, muss its sheets. Let's pretend the weight of a head also rested on one of those pillows.

10.

Quizá fue la premura al ver los últimos granos dearena traspasar esa cristalina cintura de avispa. No somos responsables de la destrucción de los muebles, sino víctimas del cuestionable gusto de un decorador de moteles baratos por haber elegido una mesilla de patas tan frágiles, incapaz de soportar el peso de dos que se mueven al ritmo del péndulo.

10.

Perhaps it was the urgency after seeing those last grains of sand drop past the hourglass' wasp-waist. We cannot be held accountable for damaging the furniture, but are instead victims of the questionable taste of a decorator of cheap motels for having chosen a table with legs so fragile, they couldn't bear the weight of two who moved to the rhythm of a pendulum.

11.

Según el Pequeño Larousse, **nervudo** te viene perfecto. *adj. Se dice de la hoja que tiene los nervios muy salientes. 2. Del cuerpo que tiene las venas, tendones y arterias muy marcados.*

11.

According to Wikipedia, **vascularity** suits you perfectly. *noun. Vascularity, in bodybuilding, is the condition of having many highly-visible, prominent, and often extensively-ramified superficial veins. [...]*

12.

Para que tu mirada no se incomode, he pasado las noches en vela memorizando un tratado anatómico cuyo contenido incluye un estudio de poses que disimulan. En sus últimas páginas he agregado un rarísimo apéndice sobre perspectivas embusteras y otro acerca de ángulos que hasta los contorsionistas más aptos envidiarían. Así he conseguido engendrar esa inestabilidad volumétrica que te devuelve la calma. A falta de atenuadores de luz cambiaré todos los focos. Sé que prefieres los de 35 watts a los de 50. Todo con tal de facilitarte el orgasmo. La metamorfosis como señuelo. Claroscuros. Suspensorios. Carnada. De pie frente a ti se presenta una silueta de músculos púberes con la esperanza de no exacerbar la indecisión que tus hormonas procuran. Tú no me creas ni me destruyes, únicamente me transformas.

12.

I've spent sleepless nights memorizing an anatomical treatise whose contents include a study of poses to conceal certain parts of the body so you don't feel uncomfortable when looking at me. In its final pages I've added a most-rare appendix on deceitful perspectives and another about angles that even the most adept contortionist would envy. This is how I've managed to conceive the bodily adjustments that calm you down. Lacking light dimmers, I will change all the bulbs. I know you prefer 35 watts instead of 50. All to facilitate your orgasm. Metamorphosis as lure. Chiaroscuros. Jockstraps. Bait. Standing before you I offer a silhouette of adolescent muscles, hoping to not exacerbate the indecision your hormones tend to resort to. You neither create nor destroy me, you only transform me.

13.

Debajo de mi piel, pero encima de tus huesos. En lo subterráneo, mas no en lo profundo, me hablas de futuros que en otros sitios prefieres callar. Mi oreja es la continuación de tus labios.

13.

Beneath my skin, but above your bones. In the subterranean, but not in the deepest regions, you speak to me of futures that in other places you prefer to keep secret. My ear is an extension of your lips.

14.

Y yo mordiéndote los hombros debajo de tu peso. Y tú aplastándome la yugular con la nariz. Acomodo la pierna para que no obstaculice tus caprichos atléticos. El flujo sanguíneo comprometido. Nunca tuvimos que oler el aroma del látex. Somos lo que dicen: mamíferos sin arreglo.

14.

As I was biting your shoulders under your weight, you were crushing my jugular with your nose. I'd shift my leg so as not to block your athletic compulsions. Risking our bloodstreams, we never smelled the scent of latex. We are what they say: incorrigible mammals.

15.

El corte transversal que suele representar al aparato reproductor es el dibujo anatómico más inexacto porque nunca queda ilustrada la manera en la que el esfínter se convierte en anillo de compromiso.

15.

The cross section that usually represents the reproductive system is the most inaccurate anatomical drawing because it never reveals the way in which the sphincter becomes an engagement ring.

16.

Háblame muy quedo. Bruma en la garganta. Que no escuchen los otros las piedras de tu voz. Sólo de susurros se alimentan los amantes anoréxicos y en público no se pueden comparar las teorías del hambre con la permanencia voluntaria, el único nutriente capaz de sostenerlos.

16.

Speak to me very softly. Mist in the throat. Don't let others hear the stones in your voice. Only on whispers do anorexic lovers feed and in public they can't compare the theories of hunger with voluntary permanence, the sole nutrient able to sustain them.

17.

Favor de no molestar, fue lo último que pudimos decirle al mundo aquel fin de semana antes de amurallarnos. Afuera, como si no existiera la playa.

17.

Please Do Not Disturb, was the last thing we were able to tell the world that weekend before barricading ourselves. It was as if the beach no longer existed outside.

18.

Este oficio de traducirte la carne. En su piel se encuentra codificada la biósfera del planeta. El pecho es un par de montañas divididas a causa de un cañón abismal y el abdomen un desierto formado por dunas idénticas. La tundra se extiende en el rostro, como un invierno perpetuo, tan blanco, casi de hielo. Las axilas guardan la humedad de un bosque en el trópico y el sexo es una selva de animales exóticos y raíces jugosas, donde llueve todo el año.

18.

This role of translating everything into your flesh. The planet's biosphere is found codified in your skin. Your chest is a pair of mountains divided by an abysmal canyon and the abdomen a desert formed of identical dunes. A tundra extends across your face, like eternal winter, so white and ice-like. Your armpits guard the wetness of a tropical forest and your sex is a jungle of exotic animals and juicy roots, where it rains all year round.

19.

Mediante exhalaciones e inhalaciones, a destiempo, así amenizamos el silencio nocturno. Sin darnos cuenta nuestro jadear arrítmico sacude el polvo acumulado sobre los muebles, sobre nosotros. Las rodillas me duelen, los codos no. Bienvenida sea la erosión del cuerpo que tu lengua provoca.

19.

Through exhalations and inhalations, out of sync, that's how we enliven the nocturnal silence. Without realizing it, our arrhythmic panting shakes the dust that's settled upon the furniture, upon ourselves. My knees hurt, but not my elbows. Welcome is this erosion of my body by your tongue.

20.

Esternocleidomastoideo. El tuyo, claro. Una palabra consigue evocarte. Una palabra también puede ser un poema.

20.

Sternocleidomastoid. Yours, of course. One word manages to remind me of you. One word can also be a poem.

21.

No existe mejor mueble que una persona. Los omóplatos pueden ser agarraderas. Descansabrazos, las plantas de los pies. Puedo ser una mesa, un taburete para tus tobillos cansados o un perchero del que puedes colgar las camisetas impregnadas con el sudor limpio de tus axilas. Te prefiero en las blancas, ceñidas, de cuello redondo, Fruit of the Loom.

21.

There is no better piece of furniture than a person. The shoulder blades can become handles. Armrests, the soles of the feet. I can turn myself into a table, a stool for your tired ankles, or a hanger from which you can hang the t-shirts impregnated with the sweet sweat of your armpits. I prefer you in the white ones, tight fitting, crew-necked, Fruit of the Loom.

22.

Como el brazo que entra en la manga de una camisa, así el meñique desaparece en el precipicio/prepucio. Sus nudillos permanecen guardados, vestidos con el excedente cutáneo tras devorar la falange.

22.

Like an arm entering the sleeve of a shirt, that's how my pinky disappears into your foreskin's many folds. Its knuckles remain tucked away, dressed in that excess skin after devouring the phalange.

23.

Si bien la decapitación fotográfica resguardaría tu dentidad y el algodón blanco tu obsequiosa genética, siempre me incomodó la posibilidad de ver tu entrepierna repetida ad nauseam en almacenes departamentales, catálogos de temporada, supermercados y panorámicos.

23.

Even if photographic decapitation would safeguard your identity and
the white cotton your generous genetics, I was always unsettled by the
possibility of seeing your crotch repeated ad nauseam in department
stores, seasonal catalogs, supermarkets and on billboards.

24.

No salgas tan deprisa a esa noche oscura. Quédate conmigo en el interior de este capullo. Porque del otro lado de esa puerta uno necesita alas, aguijones y extremidades callosas para defenderse. Caparazones. De éste nos basta con ser larvas.

24.

Don't depart in such a hurry into the dark night. Stay here with me inside this cocoon. Because on the other side of that door one needs wings, stingers, and calloused extremities to defend oneself. Exoskeletons. On this side, we can just remain as larvae.

25.

Lo más peligroso fue tu saliva. Tan cautivante. Un círculo trazado con azúcar alrededor de una mina antipersona.

25.

Your greatest danger was your saliva. So captivating. Like a circle traced with sugar around an anti-personnel mine.

II.
Destruction of the Lover

Here is the repeated image of the lover destroyed.

–Richard Siken, *Crush*

26.

Lamentablemente de nosotros sólo quedan los escombros. Pero si algún día la nostalgia te sorprende y decides buscarlos, con gusto dibujaré en un mapa la ruta que te llevará a husmear los rincones donde esas ruinas permanecen amontonadas, sin que nuestras madres lo sepan.

26.

Of us, regrettably, only the ruins remain. But if one day a bout of melancholy catches you by surprise and you decide to go search for them, I'll willingly draw on a map the route that will lead you to explore the nooks and crannies where that rubble remains piled up, without our mothers ever realizing it.

27.

Te presté una camisa estampada con cuadros blancos y azules. Me la regresaste sudada. Saberla colgada en el tubo del clóset me devolvía la calma cuando salías de viaje. Su aroma era un bálsamo a mitad de la noche capaz de disminuir mi creciente ansiedad. Por ejemplo, dedos tamborileando la mesa o el muslo. Solía olfatearla para tranquilizarme, hasta que un día mi madre la metió en la lavadora. Yo entonces dormía, sin saber que un ciclo de lavado te despedazaba con la furia centrífuga de sus aspas. Te enjuagaba. Te exprimía. Y por si acaso habían quedado rastros de ti, te volvía a enjuagar. Al drenaje se fueron tus feromonas. Ni tu cadáver pude inhalar en el filtro atrapa-pelusa. Comencé a morderme las uñas apenas el aire dejó de arrastrarte.

27.

I loaned you a white-and-blue-checkered shirt. You gave it back to me impregnated with your sweat. Knowing it was hanging in the closet helped me to calm down when you were away on trips. Its scent was a balm in the middle of the night, able to diminish my growing anxiety. For example, fingers drumming on a table or my thigh. I used to sniff it to calm myself down, until one day my mother stuck it in the washing machine. I was sleeping then, unaware that a wash cycle was ripping you to shreds with the centrifugal fury of its blades. It rinsed you. It squeezed you dry. And just in case any traces of you remained, it rinsed you once more. All of your pheromones went down the drain. I couldn't even smell your corpse in the lint filter. I began to bite my nails as soon as the air stopped carrying you.

28.

En medio de cada pareja flota una gota de veneno que duerme y espera a ser provocada para inflamarse y gestar el caos. Es imposible predecir cuándo ocurrirá. Los síntomas son diversos. Las manos comienzan a perder el tacto, el tiempo permanece en eterna duermevela, el aire se endurece y convierte en cúpula asfixiante. Hay basura en las palabras. Hay espuma en las miradas.

28.

Between every couple there floats a droplet of poison that drowses and waits to be provoked, to become inflamed and sow chaos. It's impossible to predict when this will occur. The symptoms are varied. Hands begin to lose their touch, time remains eternally snoozing, the air hardens and becomes a suffocating cupola. Words turn into rubbish. A layer of fog overshadows sight.

29.

El agujero que deja tu forma durante su ausencia, es la amargura. Andar de animal enfermo negándose a surtir labores lácteas. Proyecto divino varado en las playas de tus muslos. Semen buscándose en las bocas. Sangre buscándose en la sangre.

29.

The void left by your body during its absence is pure bitterness. Like the pacing of an ailing animal refusing to suckle its young. A divine project run aground on the beaches of your thighs. Semen searching for itself in other mouths. Blood searching for itself in the bloodstreams of others.

30.

Mientras tu mirada se nubla, la mía permanece sembrada en la oscuridad de la alcoba y trata de distinguir, entre las heladas aristas del mobiliario, lo único orgánico: el perfil de tu rostro, su amenazante mandíbula. Ese filo que de pronto se vuelve cuello: navaja. Hacia el sur se accidenta. Y yo ya no sé si el combustible que alimenta a este insomnio se debe a que presagio el final de los tiempos o a no querer dejar de peinarte los músculos con las uñas. Que nadie me obligue a pronunciar en voz alta la palabra *despierta* cuando te encuentres soñando.

30.

As your gaze clouds over, mine remains alert in the darkness of the room and tries to distinguish, among the sharp edges of the furnishings, the only organic thing: the profile of your face, its threatening jawline. That blade that suddenly becomes neck: razor. Further south there's a shift. And I no longer know if the fuel that feeds this insomnia is due to my foreseeing the end of our time or my not wanting to stop combing your muscles with my nails. Let nobody force me to speak aloud the word *awake* when you're dreaming.

31.

Domar a nuestro orgasmo me fastidia. Someter a sus gritos a un constante adelgazamiento para convertirlos en gemidos famélicos, apenas audibles, débiles de tan subyugados. No consiguen traspasar ni a los muros hechos de tabla-roca. Otras veces prefieres disimularlos con el lloriqueo de una protagonista huérfana en busca de amor o con las explosiones de una película de Schwarzenegger. Depende del canal y la hora.

31.

Taming our orgasm annoys me. Subjecting its shouts to a constant restraint to turn them into famished moans, barely audible, weak from such subjugation. They can't even be heard through thin walls made of sheetrock. Other times you prefer to disguise them with the whimpering of an orphaned film star searching for love or the explosions of some Schwarzenegger film. It all depends on the channel and the time.

32.

Aunque la memoria intente llenar el espacio que alguna vez tu cuerpo ocupó, ambos sabemos que ahí sólo flotan, en una atmósfera de elementos enrarecidos, partículas diminutas de polvo sometidas a la penumbra, tan sólo perceptibles cuando la luz del día atraviesa el vidrio de la ventana. Tu existencia está en otra parte.

32.

Although my memory tries to fill the space your body once occupied, we both know that floating there, in an atmosphere of rarified elements, are just miniscule particles of dust subdued by the penumbra, perceivable only when sunlight crosses the windowpane. Your existence is elsewhere.

33.

Dante olvidó cartografiar en su Infierno la circunferencia donde penarán los metrosexuales.

33.

Dante forgot to chart in his Inferno the circle where metrosexuals will be punished.

34.

Este oficio de interpretar a la carne. Anoche te vi en un museo. Me mordí los labios hasta sangrar frente al guardia cuando logré reconocer tu pecho, tus muslos. Las tetillas idénticas. Tus ingles. Los testículos, casi. La misma mandíbula. Un clon de mármol encima de un pedestal.

34.

This role of interpreting your flesh. Last night I saw you in a museum. I bit my lips until they bled in front of the guard when I managed to recognize your chest, your thighs. The nipples were identical. It was your groin. The testicles, nearly so. The same jaw. A clone made of marble atop a pedestal.

35.

Cuando desperté, tu cuerpo todavía estaba allí. Éramos fósiles.

35.

When I woke, your body was still there. We were fossils.

36.

Qué pesadilla (o lo que Nostradamus no pudo). Anoche soñé que en tu cuarto de baño colgaban del tubo dos toallas. Sólo una de ellas tenía bordada la palabra *Él* con hilaza celeste.

36.

What a nightmare (what Nostradamus couldn't prophesize). Last night I dreamed that in your bathroom two towels hung from the rod. Only one of them was embroidered with the word *His* in blue thread.

37.

De mis ojos a tus ojos, el calvario. De tu piel a mi boca, el abismo. Los silencios. Las paredes. Una incómoda lejanía milimétrica. Entre las sábanas sólo queda de tu historia la histeria. De mi historia el misterio. Las voces. Otras lenguas cansadas de buscarse. Los disfraces. Un montón de piedras invisibles. El instinto ronda a solas en el estallido de muros.

37.

From my eyes to your eyes, the torment. From your skin to my mouth, the abyss. The silences. The walls. An uncomfortable millimetric distance. Between the sheets, only the hysteria remains of your history. Of my history, the mystery. The voices. Other tongues tired of searching for you. The disguises. A pile of invisible stones. Instinct prowls alone in the shattering of walls.

38.

Cuando me la presentaste le besé una mejilla y al instante pude reconocer en las cuarteaduras de su maquillaje estropeado la inequívoca fragancia de una eyaculación reciente amenizándole el pómulo.

38.

When you introduced her to me I kissed her on the cheek and could immediately recognize in the cracks of her patched makeup the unmistakable scent of a recent ejaculation enlivening her cheek.

39.

Cariño,

Nadie me entregó un mapa para que te siguiera al bosque en el que deambulas libremente. Estoy perdiendo tu aroma.

39.

Honey,

No one handed me a map to follow you into the forest where you roam unfettered. I'm losing your scent.

40.

Cuando por fin decidas husmear los escombros, no te será muy difícil hallar encajado en la grieta de algún muro, o quizá debajo de una silla desvencijada, este cuaderno de auxilios nocturnos en el cual registré tus múltiples construcciones y destrucciones. En sus páginas ha quedado escrita una historia que no pudo ser. La que prefirió omitir nuestros nombres. La que perpetuará su indeciso equilibrio en las puntas de dos lenguas.

40.

When at last you decide to sniff out the ruins, it won't be very difficult for you to find embedded in the crack of some wall, or perhaps beneath some rickety chair, this notebook of nocturnal aid in which I have registered your multiple constructions and destructions. Its pages contain in writing a story that couldn't survive. The one that chose to omit our names. The one that shall remain in an indecisive balance on the tips of two tongues.

41.

Esta noche incendiaré nuestro lecho. Que no quede rastro alguno. Tú y yo siempre conservaremos un alfabeto tatuado con tinta escarlata bajo la ropa.

41.

I shall burn our bed tonight. Let no trace of us remain. You and I will always retain an alphabet tattooed in scarlet ink beneath our clothes.

ABOUT THE AUTHOR

Luis Panini (Monterrey, México, 1978) is a writer and architect. He is the author of six novels: *Esquirlas (27 editores/UANL, 2014), El uranista (Tusquets, 2014), La hora mala (Tusquets, 2016), Los Cronopolios I. Las Espirales del Tiempo (Destino, 2016), Los Cronopolios II. Las oscuridad paralela (Destino, 2017) and Los Cronopolios III. La noche infinita (Destino, 2018); four collections of short fiction: Terrible anatómica (Conarte, 2009), Mala fe sensacional (Fondo Editorial Tierra Adentro, 2010), Función de repulsa (Libros Malaletra, 2015) and Retrovisor (Atrasalante/Conarte, 2018); one children's book: Una cabeza distinta (Petra Ediciones, 2018); and one poetry Destrucción del amante (UANL, 2016).* He won the Nuevo León Literature Prize in 2008 for his first book. A graduate in architecture from the UANL, he completed his postgraduate studies at the University of Kentucky and the Herbstakademie in Germany. He belongs to Mexico's Sistema Nacional de Creadores de Arte and lives in Los Angeles.

ABOUT THE TRANSLATOR

Lawrence Schimel is a bilingual poet and translator of poetry, working in and between Spanish and English. His translations of poetry appear regularly in many international magazines and journals, including *Modern Poetry in Translation*, *Writers Without Borders*, *Latin American Literature Today*, *PN Review*, *Pleiades*, *The Brooklyn Rail*, *Agenda*, *Río Grande Review*, *Structo*, etc. Other Mexican poetry collections he's translated include *Dangerous Matter* by Gabriela Cantú Westendarp (Literal Publishing), *I'd ask you to join me by the Río Bravo to weep but you should know neither tears nor river remain* by Jorge Humberto Chávez (Shearsman), *Bomarzo* by Elsa Cross (Shearsman, forthcoming), and *Hamartia* by Carmen Boullosa (White Pine Press, forthcoming).

ALSO AVAILABLE FROM THE
PLEIADES PRESS TRANSLATION SERIES

30 Questions People Don't Ask
Poems by Inga Gaile, translated by Ieva Lešinska

The Olive Trees' Jazz & Other Poems
by Samira Negrouche, translated by Marilyn Hacker

PLEIADES
P R E S S